Shamanic

DEPOSSESSION

And Other True

Healing Miracles

Also by Brad "Little Frog" Hudson:

Vision Quests: True Stories From the Wilderness

The Truth About You: Who You Are and Why You're Here on Earth

Shamanic

DEPOSSESSION

And Other True

Healing Miracles

BRAD "LITTLE FROG" HUDSON

Little Frog Publishing
Westford, Massachusetts
2014

First Printing: 2014

ISBN 978-0-9908368-0-3

Little Frog Publishing
35 Carlisle Road
Westford, MA 01886

www.LittleFrogHealing.com

Ordering Information:

Special discounts are available on quantity purchases by corporations, associations, educators, and others. For details, contact the publisher at the above listed address.

U.S. trade bookstores and wholesalers: Please contact Little Frog Publishing at 978-590-0186 or email LittleFrogHealing@gmail.com.

For my mother, Nancy, whose passing started me on my spiritual journey.

Contents

FOREWORD

The stories that follow are all true. They have nothing to do with magic, or special powers and abilities. Rather, they document ancient knowledge that has been used by mankind for tens of thousands of years to heal physical ailments. Ancient knowledge that, for most of Western society, was discarded and lost, piece by piece, over the past two thousand years as the emergence of Christianity, the Renaissance, the Industrial Revolution and Modern Medicine took control of our lives.

There still exist in many societies around the world shamans who are responsible for the health of their fellow tribesmen. They reach out and use the same healing power I use on a daily basis. This power comes from All That Is, the Great Mystery, the Creator, the Source, or whatever you want to call the One who created everything. This healing energy is also known as Love. You can call it Reiki, or higher dimensional frequencies, or a million other names, but at its core it's all Love in its many different forms.

The world is changing. Quantum physics and shamanism at first glance appear an odd couple, but shamanism is helping modern physicists to better understand the strange world of quantum particles. Doctors are beginning to take note of alternative healing modalities because they produce positive results. Humanity is finally re-awakening to the benefits of shamanic culture.

Anyone with training and practice can do what I do as a shamanic healer. This is my primary message. I am not special.

We are all born with these abilities. Collectively as a society we decided long ago to forgo this route. The good news is that this decision is now being reversed. Interest in shamanism and other alternative healing modalities continues to grow briskly year after year.

I encourage you to learn more about shamanism. Take the weekend workshop on basic shamanism given by the Foundation for Shamanic Studies. Contact a local shaman and ask about learning how to journey.

You will discover a wonderful circle of new friends and a new way of looking at the world.

You won't be disappointed.

Brad "Little Frog" Hudson
Westford, MA
June 2014

INTRODUCTION

Depossession work is not for the faint of heart.

The first time I heard about depossession work I knew it was for me. I've always been the type of guy who hates bullies. I was the guy in school who stood up for the kids being harassed for their lunch money. I was never afraid to speak up and act if needed. When I first learned that spirits can invade the living, I made it my mission to find out more.

But what I found out is that not every possessing spirit is a bully. Actually, most are "suffering beings", a term I initially heard while taking Betsy Bergstrom's Compassionate Depossession Intensive. The majority of the spirits inside living people are there because they are scared and don't realize they are dead. They are looking for refuge, someplace safe. They don't realize they are draining the life force from the person they are occupying. These spirits just want help so they can go home.

Some of the suffering beings had severe problems while alive and seek out similar living people when they die. They aren't ready to cross over, so they take up residence within someone with the same problem they had, like drugs, alcohol, or violent behavior. This makes them feel at home.

Another class of possessing spirits are the truly malevolent spirits. Most of these beings are ancient and not from this Earth. They feed on negative energy and emotions, like anger and hate. The more upset the host is, the stronger the being becomes. Oftentimes these beings incite their unwilling host to kill other people or themselves- the "voices in my head" heard by those unfortunate enough to fall victim to their thoughts. I have discovered that many times this occurs because the occupying being is so old it does not remember how to cross over, and instead wants to follow another soul home upon death.

Sometimes the being doesn't leave. I've had experiences where, no matter what I've done, I cannot get the spirit to move on. I've ruled out thought forms and curses. In these cases, I've found that many times the living person doesn't want the spirit to leave, no matter what they tell me. A strange sort of symbiotic relationship develops that I do not understand. These people I cannot help.

The final type of possession I've found is called the "drop in". This is when the soul born into a body wants to leave physical incarnation early, and finds a replacement soul to take over the body. This is a rare occurrence.

The good news is that most depossession work is simple and straightforward. If the being presents itself, it wants help. It wants to cross over, it just doesn't know how to cross. A few simple actions, and they are gone for good. The person who was possessed feels better immediately, and the work is done.

Depossession work scares most people, including many lightworkers. They fear it because they don't fully understand it. Fear is the ultimate limiting belief. With proper training and protection, anyone can depossess other people from the spirits inside them. It is a simple procedure. It is a wonderful experience to help a frightened, suffering being cross over and find its way back home.

Shamanic Depossession

CHAPTER ONE
A MALEVOLENT POSSESSION

The subject line of the email read, "EMERGENCY!" The message was "I am in urgent need of a shaman. URGENT!!" No name, just a phone number.

It was the Friday before Thanksgiving, and I was checking my emails after dinner. My initial thought was someone was pulling my leg. I would expect more info if it was truly an emergency; heck a name at the very least. Then I noticed the email was forwarded from the Foundation for Shamanic Studies website where I am listed as a Shamanic Practitioner in Massachusetts. Maybe this IS serious after all.

I called the number and spoke with a near-hysterical woman, Judy, who told me her son needed immediate help, NOW! She explained that John, in his late twenties, was possessed by an "evil spirit" she called the "Tall Man". The Tall Man was 8 feet tall, wore a long black cloak, and had no face. She and her son began seeing this spirit over ten years ago when they lived across the street from a cemetery. The Tall Man followed them when they moved, and slowly took over John's body.

Judy said this spirit was responsible for her son's heroin addiction, and his many suicide attempts over the past few years. She described her son as always angry at everyone. His health was deteriorating rapidly. Not surprising news because this type of spirit feeds on the negative energy created by anger, and manifests as a wasting away of the client's body. This particular night Judy was very frightened, because as she was preparing to take her son to the hospital he disappeared from the house. She had no idea where he was or what he was doing. She was thinking the worst had happened.

Judy asked me if I could begin work on John immediately. I explained that as a shaman I must have explicit permission from the client to work on him. Working on a person without his or her permission is sorcery in the eyes of a shaman. Judy was struggling with that bit of information when John walked into the house. I was able to speak directly with John, and obtained his permission after I explained what I would try to do for him.

Judy then explained she was committing her son to the psychiatric ward at her local hospital that evening, and asked me to come work on him the next day. However I was attending a shamanic workshop on death and dying that weekend in Rhode Island, so the earliest I could possibly visit John would be the following Monday. While Judy wasn't happy with my answer, she accepted my offer to work on John remotely in the meantime. I've performed long distance depossessions in the past, but always with non-malevolent spirits. I wondered how this one would play out.

I tried a few healing techniques that night with no discernible results other than an increase in John's anger, according to Judy. She was talking to him every hour via cell phone. I told her my next opportunity to work on John would be Sunday.

The perfect opportunity to work on John remotely presented itself during the last exercise of the class on Sunday afternoon. The exercise was to journey to a deceased person and help that spirit cross over into the Light. I knew instantly that I would be contacting the Tall Man, and I was anxious to get going.

I journeyed to the Lower World and met my primary power animal, Shadow. I surrounded us with a protective bubble of love (i.e. white light), and I asked Shadow to take me to the Tall Man. A second later I was standing in front of him, Shadow by my side. He was not at all pleased to see me.

"What are you doing here, shaman?" he asked.

"I've come to help you get to a better place" I answered.

"Get away from me, you pest!" he spat. And with that the verbal assault began. At the same time I was trying to find a way to hold him long enough to have Shadow take us to the Light, the Tall Man was trying to enter my spirit body. The protective layer of love I put around myself blocked each attempt. This made the Tall Man very angry. Suddenly it was time to return; the journey was over. As I departed the Tall Man yelled after me, "I'll get you for this! I will make your life miserable!"

That evening I received a call from Judy. She told me that John called her, telling her that the Tall Man was extremely upset and yelling at him "Get that shaman away from me!" Neither Judy nor John knew that I made direct contact with the spirit earlier that day. Judy was very concerned that this escalation would somehow harm John. I promised to visit John in the hospital the next day.

When I woke up the following morning, the Tall Man wasted no time - he was in my head attacking me immediately. He swore at me, and told me all the horrible things he was going to do to me once he entered my body. I was careful not to argue with him or try to fight him as this would only make him stronger. At first it was a minor inconvenience; after an hour of this I was pretty much fed up with him. At that point I politely told him I had heard enough of his rants, so I put up a protective shield of love around my body. In an instant he was gone- there was no way he could enter my psychic field through the shield. I then prepared for my visit to John.

I arrived at the hospital after a ninety minute drive, which gave me plenty of time to plan my approach and encircle myself with another protective sphere of love. I reached out to the Angels of the Light, who are instrumental in these depossessions, and asked them to be ready to assist me when I call on them.

Only immediate family members and clergy have visiting privileges in the psychiatric ward. I am an ordained minister of the Circle of the Sacred Earth Church, so I was permitted access to John, although I did have to leave my personal belongings at the security desk.

Before I walked into John's room, I put myself in a space of pure love. Depossessions are all about empathy and love for the suffering being within the client. All my attention is focused upon helping the spirit get to where he belongs in the kindest way possible.

"Hi John, I'm Brad, the shaman your Mom told you about. You and I spoke on the phone the other night" I said. I explained what I was planning, namely removing the Tall Man from his body and helping him cross into the Light. First I had to make contact with the Tall Man.

I asked John if the Tall Man was in the room with us. He wasn't sure. He looked around the room but said he didn't see him. I was sure I could feel the Tall Man's presence, and that was a very good sign- if the spirit shows up, it means he wants help no matter what he says during the course of the depossession.

"OK, John, I'd like you to move your consciousness to one side in your head and let your mind go blank. I'm going to try to establish a dialogue with the Tall Man, Just say the first thing that pops into your mind after each question" I explained. John was willing to give it a try.

"Is the Tall Man here with us?" I asked.

"Yes" replied John, somewhat slowly. His voice was different.

I mustered as much love as I could. "Thank you for answering" I said. "My name is Brad, and it is a real pleasure to meet you. What is your name?"

"Marcus" he answered. Aha, contact established- a very good sign!

"Hi Marcus. I'm very interested in knowing more about you if you don't mind. How old are you?" I asked.

"I don't know" was the reply.

I asked if he was 400, 500, or 1,000 years old.

"Very old" he said.

"Where were you born?" I inquired.

"I don't remember" said Marcus.

I asked if he was born on Earth.

"No" was his one word reply.

Now I know I am dealing with an ancient being from another world. Good start. It is always beneficial to know what type of entity I'm trying to help.

John appeared to be in a trance-like state, which was perfect for letting Marcus through.

"Marcus, are you with any other humans they way you are with John?" I asked.

"Yes" said Marcus.

I asked how many others.

"Five" was the reply. Now it's even more important for me to get Marcus to the Light- four other people will benefit from this!

"Marcus, do you know what the word "happy" means?" I asked.

"Yes" he replied.

"Are you happy Marcus?" I inquired. No answer from Marcus- but that, too, was a good sign. No answer is the same as a yes when doing this work.

"Would you like to be happy, Marcus? Can you remember being happy?" I asked. Still no answer from Marcus. That's a big green light for me.

"Marcus, do you have a heart?" I asked, continuing my questioning.

"No" he replied.

"Marcus, everyone has a heart" I answered. "Just because you're very old and unhappy doesn't mean you don't have a heart. The Creator gave every one of us a heart when we were born, no matter when or where we were born. Your heart may have shriveled up into a tiny little hard ball over the eons, but you still have one."

No reply from Marcus.

I kept going. "Marcus, do you know what an Angel is?" I asked hopefully.

"Yes" came his reply.

I followed with "Do you mind if I call in an Angel to be with us?" No answer, so I reached out to one of the Angels of the LIght who was standing by, and asked him to come in and hover above John's head.

"Marcus, can you see the angel who just joined us?" I asked.

"Yes" was the reply.

"Marcus, do you know what love is?" I asked. No answer.

I followed with "Do you mind if I ask this Angel to beam some love into your heart?" Still no answer- a good sign. I mentally asked the Angel to begin beaming love into Marcus' heart. I waited a minute, and when Marcus made no protestations, I asked three more Angels of the Light to join us and beam even more love into Marcus.

This Angelic injection of love makes spirits buoyant, and causes them to float. I noticed that Marcus was floating, and asked him if he could feel it.

"Yes" he replied.

I was pleased to see that Marcus wasn't going to fight the process. To the contrary, he seemed relieved and welcomed it.

"Now, Marcus, when the Angels have lifted you out of John's body, they will take you to the Light so you can experience happiness and love and live your true life. You will be totally safe the entire time. Are you ready?" I asked.

Marcus nodded yes.

I mentally asked the Angels to take Marcus to the Light and help him cross. About ten seconds later I heard in my head, "He has crossed". I extended my senses throughout the hospital room and could no longer feel Marcus' presence.

I asked John to come back.

"John, do you remember anything that just happened?"

John replied, "No, except for this funny feeling that something was lifted from me. It felt like a big helium balloon just rose out of me."

I explained how the Angels lifted Marcus out of his body and carried him to the Light, where he crossed over. "He won't be coming back" I said. John sighed with relief.

I spent the next hour doing additional healing on John. I removed the cords of attachment that Marcus left behind. When I completed the healing, I taught him how to protect himself with Love. Love is the most powerful force in the universe. Everything was and is created by Love.

I explained to John that he still has holes in his spirit body, and these will heal in time as his physical body is healed. In the meantime, he needs to be overly cautious about protecting himself while he gets his life back together.

Finally, after nearly three hours with John, I felt comfortable leaving. I had done all I could for him.

Judy called me five days later and told me that John was released from the hospital and was in a drug rehabilitation program getting his life back together. The anger and other emotional issues related to Marcus were almost completely absent from his life. They were both very grateful.

When I hung up the phone, I cried from joy and relief. I thanked Spirit for allowing me to be a part of John's healing process. Spirit helped me help John. Together we were able to do what modern medicine was unable to do for John.

CHAPTER TWO:
A MALEVOLENT POSSESSION PART TWO

I received a phone call on a Sunday night in early August from Judy. I had not heard from her in nine months. I could hear the concern and anxiety in her voice immediately.

"Hi Brad, I hope I'm not disturbing you."

"Hi Judy, no not at all. This is a surprise! What's up?"

"It's John," she said. "There's something wrong with him again. Can I have him explain it to you? He's standing right here."

"Sure," I replied. "Please put him on."

"Hi Brad," said John. "I'm hearing voices again. They tell me to kill myself. And there are all these beings in black hoods around me."

"How long has this been going on?" I asked.

"A few weeks now. They either tell me to kill myself, or they tell me to kill someone else."

"What do they look like?" I inquired.

"They wear these black hoods, like capes with hoods, and they don't have any faces. It's just black where their faces should be."

John sounded much stronger than the John I met nine months earlier. "John, you sound really good compared to last time man."

"Yeah, I was feeling good until this happened. Getting my life back together. Now these things showed up."

"OK, I'm getting a message that these beings are lost. They don't remember how to cross over to get home. So they are using you, trying to get you to kill yourself or someone else in order to follow the deceased's soul to the Light," I explained. "Can you hang in there for two or three more days?"

"Yeah, I think I can do that," replied John.

"Great! Can you put your mother back on the phone please?"

I explained to Judy that the earliest I could make it to her house was on Wednesday. We agreed to meet at 4:30pm, after she got home from work.

That night I had an incredible dream. I dreamt I was a huge warrior, ten feet tall, like a super-sized Conan the Barbarian, standing inside the courtyard area of a rundown ancient castle. Demons and other malevolent beings were attacking me from all directions, and I was defending myself from their blows, grabbing them and throwing them against walls and columns. And I was having the time of my life! I was laughing out loud as I grabbed one after another of the creatures and threw them through stone walls. I felt exhilarated! I defeated them without a scratch on me. I took this as a good sign for Wednesday.

I arrived at Judy's house a little late; the drive was over an hour and the traffic was heavy. The first thing I saw when I entered her house was the incredible quantity of pill containers on her dining room table. There were at least twenty, maybe twenty five containers, each containing a different pill.

"Holy cow!" I exclaimed. "Does John take all of these pills?"

"Yep," Judy replied. "He is bi-polar, so half of them are his standard prescriptions. The rest he was recently given for the voices he was hearing."

"OK, that explains the beings," I said. "the drugs for the bi-polar issue by themselves are enough to cause serious holes in his energy body. These beings look for holes, which allow them to enter a person's body.

"The good thing is that John didn't have any problems for the past nine months. That tells me these beings are looking for a way home. They know I helped the Tall Man get home through John, so they may have entered John because they know I can help them."

At that point John entered the living room, and he looked great. He had put on a little weight, losing the starved look he had last time I saw him, and his skin was no longer pasty white. His eyes were clear. It was obvious John was working hard on his journey to recovery.

17

"Hey John, good to see you man!" I said.

"Yeah, you too," he replied as we shook hands.

"You look great! I hear you're working hard to get your life together."

"Yeah, it's a long road man."

"OK, what do you say we get right to work?"

I asked John to sit on the sofa, and I grabbed a dining room chair so I could sit directly opposite him. I explained the procedure to him, the same thing we did none months earlier. I asked him to move his consciousness to the side, and answer my questions with the very first thing that came into his mind. That will be the beings answering.

I realized that the palms of my hands were throbbing. Generally they only get this way when I'm working with multidimensional energies. This was new. I took it as an indication the beings were already with us, and they were strong.

I took a few deep breaths and placed myself in that space of pure Love I use for depossessions. I felt a bubble of Love surrounding the two of us, creating a safe work environment. i was just beginning to feel the presence of the hooded beings.

"Are the hooded beings with us right now?" I asked.

"Yes."

"How many of them are here?"

18

"Three"

"Are you from this Earth?"

"No."

"Where are you from?"

"Satan."

"So you are ancient beings?"

"Yes."

"My name is Brad, and I'm here to help all of you. I consider you my friends. I love each of you. Do you want to cross over?"

"Yes."

Wow, that answer took me by surprise. I wasn't expecting it to be this easy.

"Do you have a heart?"

"No."

"Actually, each of you have a heart. It's just that you are so old it has shriveled up. Do you know what angel is?"

"Yes."

"Can I call in my angel friends?"

"No."

Uh oh, maybe this won't be as easy as I thought. Time to switch gears.

"Do you know what Love is?"

"Yes."

"Do you have Love in your hearts? "

"No."

"My friends, that is not true. Everyone has Love in their hearts. The Creator created everything that exists from the energy of pure Love. Just like me, you were created with a heart full of pure Love. You may have a heart the size of a small cinder, but that heart still contains the seed of Love that you were created with."

No response.

"I'm going to call in my friends, the angels of the Light. They will not harm you in any way. They are pure Love, and are here to assist you, who are also my friends, to cross over into the Light. Is that OK?"

"Yes."

"I now call in the angels of the Light to help my three hooded friends. I ask the angels to begin beaming pure Love into the hearts of my hooded friends."

I waited a few minutes. "Do you feel the Love entering your hearts?"

"No."

Hmm. I suddenly realized that I did not call in enough angels of the Light. We are starting from scratch here, with such small, damaged hearts, that I needed more than the usual four angels. I called out for more angels, quickly! In a moment I had two dozen angels working on the hooded beings.

A few minutes later, I asked again, "Do you feel the Love entering you now?"

"Yes."

Whew! We are now in the home stretch, thankfully.

"You are now becoming buoyant from the Love the angels are filling your hearts with. Can you feel yourselves rising, my friends?"

"Yes."

"Great! Now, as you each rise out of John, a group of angels will take you into their arms very gently, and support you with their pure Love. Once you are all in the arms of the angels, they will take you to the Light and assist you with crossing over."

I waited another few minutes, until I sensed all three beings were out of John.

"My friends, all three of you are now in the arms of the angels, correct?"

"Yes."

21

"I now ask the angels to take our three friends to the Light and help them cross over and go home."

With that I sensed them leave and a few seconds later I received the message from the angels that my three hooded friends were now home. I thanked the angels for their help. Time to bring John back.

"John, it's time to come back now. How do you feel?"

"I feel lighter, a lot lighter," replied John. "It felt like these things inside of me were being rolled up and leaving through my head."

I laughed. "That's exactly what you said last time I did this for you."

I realized in this moment that the bubble of pure Love that had been surrounding us was now gone. The palms of my hands were no longer throbbing. I couldn't sense any malevolent beings around us. Everything seemed normal.

"John, do you sense any beings around us?"

"Nope, everything just feels clear."

"Excellent!" I replied. I gave John some advice on how to protect himself along with specific procedures to do every day. Then I stood up and gave him a great big bear hug.

"You take care of yourself John. Keep up the terrific work you are doing on yourself. And call me immediately if this ever happens again, OK?"

"Yeah man, I will," replied John.

With that, I jumped into my car and drove home with a big smile on my face.

Shamanic Depossession

CHAPTER THREE
A LOVING POSSESSION

I received a call in late 2012 from a woman in Canada whose daughter was very sick. The daughter, Diane, first became ill in December 2011. Since then she had been in and out of hospitals, specialty clinics, and seen dozens of doctors. Modern medicine could not ascertain what was wrong with Diane. No one was able to help her. Her mother, Nancy, had a vision that if she did not get her daughter help quickly, she would die within the month. That's when she called me.

Diane's symptoms were rather vague. She was "wasting away", not eating, losing strength, no energy, all skin and bones. While her doctors were unable to formulate a diagnosis, to me it sounded like classic possession symptoms. Yet Diane made no mention of a spirit around or within her.

Diane emailed me permission to work on her. I started with a diagnostic journey to her spirit body. I journeyed to the Lower World to grab Shadow, my primary power animal, and asked Shadow to take us to Diane's spirit body. Instantly I was standing next to her holographic energy body, and I noticed immediately something wasn't quite right. I merged with Shadow for extra protection, and then began running my hands over Diane's spirit body trying to detect the abnormality I felt.

Suddenly it hit me- she had too much energy in her body! The excess energy had a different feel to it, like it wasn't part of her body. Had I discovered the being I was sure was inside of her?

I called out "Is there anyone here besides Diane?"

No answer.

I tried again. "Is there anyone else here besides Diane? I'm here to help you."

I heard a weak "Yes" reply, and suddenly I could see the faint outline of a man's body inside Diane's energy body.

"My name is Brad. What's your name?" I asked.

"Peter" came the reply. Excellent, I thought, I've made contact with the being.

"Peter, I'm here to help you" I reiterated.

"I don't want any help" was Peter's reply.

"Why don't you want my help Peter?" I inquired gently.

"I don't want to leave Diane" he replied. "She's the only person who ever loved me, and I love her, so I'm not leaving."

"It's wonderful to have someone who loves you Peter. How did you know Diane?" I asked.

"She was my girlfriend. But I committed suicide right before Christmas" he explained to me.

Now it's starting to make sense, I thought. The timing of his suicide corresponds with the period when Diane became ill.

"I'm so sorry to hear that Peter. I understand why you don't want to leave Diane. Did you know you have many loved ones waiting for you at the Light, waiting for you to cross over?"

"I'm not going anywhere. I'm staying right her with Diane. She loves me." he said firmly.

"Ok, ok, I understand that. But let me ask you something Peter. You love Diane, right?"

"Yes" he replied.

"Ok, and since you love her, you would never want to do anything that would hurt her, would you? I asked.

"No, of course not" he said.

"Peter, you are hurting Diane by staying in her body. You are draining her of her life energy. She will die soon if you don't leave her" I stated.

No reply, just silence. I continued.

"Just because you cross over doesn't mean you will never see Diane again. To the contrary, you can see her any time you want, be with her any time you want- and the best part is you won't be hurting her by visiting after crossing over" I explained.

"Really?" he asked.

"Absolutely! Not only do you get to be with all your loved ones who have already crossed, you can come back here to visit any time. You can leave signs for Diane to find so she knows you are still around. And each time she thinks of you,

you will hear her. And because you've crossed over you won't be hurting her any longer. What do you think?"

Silence. Then I heard a faint "Really?" from Peter. Obviously he was giving it deep thought.

"Here, grab my hands Peter" I asked as I extended my arms towards him. I grabbed hold of his hands and gently began pulling him out of Diane. I mentally told Shadow to be ready to get us to the Light the moment I had him extricated from Diane's spirit body.

Almost there...Ok, Shadow, NOW! I yelled in my head, and suddenly all three of us were standing at the edge of the Light. I could see the silhouettes of bodies standing there, patiently waiting for Peter.

"Ok, Peter, this is where we let you off so you can cross over" I said. I let go of Peter and watched him walk into the Light, hugging the silhouettes as he went.

I waited a few minutes, then reached out with my mind to ask "Peter, are you OK?"

"Yes, I'm fine. Thank you" was his reply.

I de-merged from Shadow, made sure I did not have any non-beneficial energies or entities attached to me, and returned to the Lower World to drop off Shadow. Then I returned to my living room where I had been sitting in my recliner the entire time. I relaxed a while, then got up and sent Nancy an email explaining what I had done with Shadow's help. She immediately called me to tell me that Diane had just eaten her first real meal in nearly three months!

Over the next few weeks Diane's health continued to improve until she was back to her normal self. Once again, I was honored and humbled to have helped a person who had seemingly run out of options to reclaim her life.

CHAPTER FOUR
THE DROP IN

I received an email via my website one evening from a woman named Susan, who was concerned about her friend Natalie.

Susan is a nurse with lots of experience working in the psychiatric wards in hospitals, so she has seen it all. But what she saw happening to her friend frightened her. Susan reached out to a shaman for help, and that shaman recommended she contact me. A few hours later, we were speaking about the problem.

Natalie was an old friend of Susan's who contracted the West Nile virus 2 years ago. She spent over a year in a coma, on life support. She was kept alive by feeding tubes and a respirator. With West Nile, you either come out of the coma, or you die. Fortunately, Natalie came out of her coma, but she is severely impaired. She is unable to walk or take care of herself, but she can talk. She is in a nursing home, and Susan visits her every couple of months.

Susan just visited her over the weekend, and she was shocked by what she saw. She said her friend's physical appearance had changed completely, so much that she barely recognized her. Natalie, who had been a plain woman all her life, was now stunningly beautiful. At one point Susan looked Natalie straight in the eyes, and she swears it wasn't Natalie looking back at her. Her first thought was, "My friend is possessed!"

I could sense the fear in Susan's voice as she talked. She gave me more information. Natalie has no living relatives. Natalie's husband passed away a few months after she recovered from her coma. This was the key that allowed me to figure out what was happening to Natalie.

I had a sense of what was going on with Natalie when I first read her email. That first hit wasn't bad, in fact it was positive, very positive. This was not your standard run of the mill possession. This was a drop in spirit.

While Natalie was in her coma, she was given a choice of coming back to her physical life or staying "home" and letting her physical body die. She chose to return to Earth, to be with her husband, and continue her life. But then a few months later her husband passed away. This was too much for Natalie, and she asked her angels to leave. She no longer wanted to complete this lifetime on Earth. So another soul volunteered to take over her physical body and allow Natalie to leave.

This is a win/win situation for both Natalie and the new spirit inhabiting her body. Natalie was able to go home to be with her departed husband and other deceased loved ones instead of suffering through a very long, and most likely incomplete, rehabilitation by herself. The new spirit is able to enter physical incarnation and experience the intense physical and mental rehabilitation after the coma, without having to have lived for 50 years first. This soul can learn valuable lessons from its experience in a very short time. So both Natalie and the new soul get what they wanted and no one but Susan knows.

Susan felt much better after we spoke. Her fear was gone. She understood that this is a good thing for Natalie. I suggested asking the new Natalie on her next visit why she swapped places with her friend. I can't wait to hear her answer!

CHAPTER FIVE
RESISTANCE

There are instances where I am unable to help my client no matter what I try. I used to think it was because the being did not want to leave the client's body. I soon learned that not every person who contacts me for assistance wants the being removed. When I am unable to help the being move from my client's body, it is because my client won't let go, no matter what my client tells me.

While on vacation at the beach I received a frantic phone call requesting help from an elderly woman. Her name was Tracy. She was talking a mile a minute, and I had to listen intently so I wouldn't miss any of the details.

"Brad I need your help!" she declared as soon as I answered my phone. "He's taken over my body and I don't know what to do! All he does is curse constantly, and berate me. He won't leave me alone!"

"Who is "he", Tracy?" I asked.

"My father, that's who. He tried controlling my life while he was alive, and now he's doing it after he's dead. Oh, all that negativity! I can't stand it! He thinks he needs to take care of me. Get him out!"

"Ok, Tracy, let's start at the beginning," I said gently. "When did this start?"

"Oh, two and a half years ago it began," she replied. "I was visiting my mother on the west coast, and he just swooped in out of nowhere and took up residence in me. I ask the angels all the time to get him out of me. I've tried everything but nothing works! Such anger and resentment, I hate it! What can I do?"

I explained I was on vacation, and wouldn't be able to work on her in person for at least a week. She lived eight hours away by car, so I needed to make some plans.

"Tracy, this is what I'm going to do. Since I cannot get to you for at least a week, I will do some exploratory journeys for you, see if I can make contact with your father and find out why he won't leave. I will figure out when I can get there, and perform a depossession in person with you. The good news is the fact that Spirit brought you to me means I can probably help you."

I listened to Tracy complain for another ten minutes before I was able to get off the phone. Wow, she was really worked up over this. I couldn't understand how she lasted over two years with his spirit inside of her. It sounded very unpleasant.

I did a journey to her father that evening. I had no trouble locating him, but he wasn't the monster that Tracy made him out to be. I wanted to make sure he knew he was dead, which he knew, and find out why he was there. I never got an answer for why he was there, the journey fizzled out at that point.

I set a date to visit Tracy. In the interim, I was receiving four to six emails from Tracy every day about how horrible her father was treating her. I felt badly that I wasn't able to help her long distance.

I was leaving to see her on a Tuesday. The Saturday before I felt awful, completely out of sorts. I couldn't figure out what was wrong, but I wasn't myself. That evening, I was sitting on my deck when suddenly I knew what was wrong with me. The previous couple of days it felt like Tracy's father was reaching out to me, annoying me with rude comments. No big deal, these kinds of things happen all the time, so I protected myself in a bubble of pure love and I was fine. But it felt like something from the father was sticking to me, a fragment of some kind. I was positive this was why I felt so bad.

What could I do about this fragment? Could I do a self-depossession? Would that work? I had never done anything like that before, but if I can help souls leave other people's bodies, surely I can do the same for my own body.

I brought myself to that place of pure love from which I conduct depossessions, called in the Angels of the Light, and began beaming Love into the fragment. Within seconds I could feel it moving up and out of me, into the waiting arms of the Angels who then took it to the Light. I felt totally normal, much different than I felt just moments before. I did it!

The next morning I received another email from Tracy, this time canceling the depossession. I wasn't surprised at all; after all, I had moved that fragment from her father from me the night before, so I was sure her father was having second thoughts about me showing up in person. It wasn't Tracy talking in that email, it was her father! I replied that I respected her wishes, and if she changes her mind I'm still available.

Tracy asked me to resume my trip the following morning, which was the day before I had planned to leave originally. I agreed, and had an uneventful drive to her home on Tuesday.

When I arrived, Tracy appeared to be in her late 70s, and quite frail. We sat outdoors in her garden. I prefer to work inside, but she insisted, so I agreed. Much like when she first called me, I couldn't get a word in edgewise. She talked nonstop about her father and how miserable he had made her life. I finally got a few words in and suggested we start working.

I asked her to move her consciousness to the side so I could establish direct contact with her father. She had a great deal of difficulty with this. Every time I asked her father a question, Tracy would answer for him. No matter how many times I asked her to stay quiet, and let her father answer, she refused.

I was getting nowhere fast. It was thirty minutes into the depossession and I hadn't made contact with the father yet. Normally I was done by now. I gave up asking questions and brought in the Angels of the Light, and asked them to beam Love into her father. Another thirty minutes passed, and still nothing. Tracy would not remain quiet. Something wasn't right.

Then Tracy's gardener showed up on her motorcycle. She parked near us and started working on the flower beds. I've had enough.

I told Tracy she wasn't letting go of her father. No matter how much she complained, I was convinced she did not want him to leave. She answered all the questions for him. I was beginning to wonder who was controlling whom at this point.

Twice while trying to communicate with her father, I heard a small, tiny voice ask "Where am I? Why am I here?" I think that was the father trying to communicate with me, but it was quickly brushed off by Tracy each time.

I told Tracy that I was absolutely sure she did not want her father's spirit to leave her. She was unwilling to participate in the depossession ritual and blocked my efforts to help her. She said she wanted him out, but her actions did not match her words.

After nearly two hours of this, I stood up to leave. Tracy continued to plead with me to help her, but there was nothing I could do until she decides she really wants her father to leave.

I had plenty of time to rethink my conclusion on the drive home. This was a big learning experience for me. It wasn't the first time my client didn't want the being to leave. And I'm sure it won't be the last time either. But it taught me to go with my instincts, my gut feeling, what my heart tells me, no matter what the client actually says.

And that is a very important lesson.

CHAPTER SIX
A LONG DISTANCE HEALING

The following healing story is quite typical of what I do nearly every day. A client contacts me, generally via email, and describes a problem he or she is experiencing. I do a journey to non-ordinary reality with one of my power animals to examine the person's spirit body and determine what I can do to help. I go to work once I get the green light from the client. Normally all my work is long distance as there is no such thing as space and time in non-ordinary reality. I've never met 95% of my clients.

Jane was referred to me by one of my friends. She wrote me an email describing her back pain and stated she has never had a full night's sleep as a result. She also mentioned problems her two grown children were experiencing, and she even mentioned a friend's problem. Could I help them?

The correct answer is never "Yes", but rather, "I'll try."

I received permission from all the parties, and I did an exploratory journey to each of their spirit bodies. While it looked like I could help Jane and her family, I wasn't sure about the friend.

Her youngest son was in rehab for a drug addiction, and Jane wanted to ensure he didn't relapse. These are difficult cases, because even though you give the client the tools they need to help themselves, you cannot guarantee the client will use them. On my first journey to him I brought Shadow, my primary power animal, and together we gave him a thorough

41

healing on a cellular level. On my next journey, I brought him Eagle. Eagle sees far and wide, nothing is hidden from Eagle. I asked Eagle to watch over him until he found his power animal. Next I taught him to do shamanic journeys, and I showed him how to find his power animal. Once he located his power animal, I thanked Eagle and released him from his work. That was all this client needed from me.

The other son had a knee injury from high school wrestling that bothered him constantly. When I journeyed to his spirit body, I knew from looking at his knee that it would take a few journeys to help him. I did four journeys with Shadow to work on him. Each time we worked on his knee I first merged with Shadow, performed the work, then de-merged and returned home. While we couldn't get his knee totally pain free, we were able to decrease the pain by 75% according to the client.

Now it was time to work on her friend's neck and back pain issues. I did a journey with Shadow and worked on her, but it didn't feel right. I got the impression we weren't helping her. Sure enough, when I received her feedback, she stated no improvement. I informed Jane I was sure I would not be able to help her friend- our vibrations just weren't matching. She needed a different person working on her. Jane insisted I do at least two more journeys for her. I performed the journeys with the same results- nothing.

Jane couldn't understand why I was able to help her sons and not her friend. I attempted to explain in five minutes what had taken me years to understand.

"We are all energy beings temporarily incarnated in physical form, and we each have a unique vibration that is like our fingerprint" I explained. " When you meet someone and get along really well with that person, your vibrations mesh together nicely. The opposite happens when you meet someone you dislike- your vibrations are not compatible. The same thing happens with healing. Some people I have no trouble helping, and others I just can't help at all. It's why there are so many alternative healing modalities. Each person gravitates towards the modality that feels right for him or her. But at the end of the day, it's the same healing energy used in each modality."

Jane's back problems were the last issue I worked on. I journeyed for her four times over two weeks. I like to wait at least three days between journeys to give the healing power time to integrate within the physical body.

At the end of the sessions, Jane told me she was no longer experiencing any back pain. For the first time in many years, she was able to sleep through the night, and go all day without her pain medication. She then mentioned that she had been diagnosed with a degenerative spine and neck condition about 30 years earlier, and this was the first non-medicated relief she ever experienced.

I had tears in my eyes as she told me this, as did she. I was quite humbled to have been a part of this miracle. It's now been two years since I worked on her, and she is still pain free!

CHAPTER SEVEN
MY PERSONAL DEPOSSESSION

Even though I had been doing depossessions for some time, a few years ago I decided to take Betsy Bergstrom's weeklong Compassionate Depossession workshop. I had decided to make depossessions the focus of my healing work, so I wanted to learn as much as possible.

I was surprised to learn that most of us have a soul or entity residing within our bodies. The vast majority of these beings are there to help and/or protect us. To prove this point, we students performed depossessions on each other for practice. Soon it was my turn to be depossessed.

The woman who volunteered to perform my depossession, Alice, confessed to me that she had no idea why she volunteered. We soon learned there was a very good reason why she volunteered.

Before Alice started, I felt tears in my eyes and a heaviness in my midsection that slowly moved up to my chest. I realized that the previous day I had not been feeling well. I was very withdrawn, non-talkative, and various old injuries were resurfacing for no apparent reason.

Alice had me relax and move my mind to one side of my head. She began asking me questions. Almost immediately I realized it was not me answering her questions. It was a being inside of me!

The being was male, and said he had been with me for over a thousand years. He was not with anyone else, just me.

He was there to protect me. Slowly the story came out. He and I were Viking warriors together, and we had a blood pact that whoever was killed in battle first would come back and protect the other. He was killed first. Evidently we had put no time limit on the protection.

Alice asked the Viking warrior if he wanted to leave. "Who will protect Brad?" he asked. Alice convinced him I could take care of myself.

Then Alice asked him if he had a belief system about death and where one goes upon death. "Valhalla" came the reply.

Alice brought in Odin and Viking warriors along with the Light. I began to feel a lifting upwards from inside of me. Alice said the Light was getting brighter, and even though my eyes were closed It was very bright around me. I could feel the being rising up out of me. After five minutes the being was completely separated from me. At that time the Viking warriors and Odin gave him a hero's welcome to Valhalla and they all disappeared into the Light.

Tears were streaming down my face. I was filled with the latent energy of the warrior who had just departed me after a thousand years of service. Alice grounded me for ten minutes to make sure all the energy was gone. I felt much lighter and my smile returned. I hugged Alice and thanked her repeatedly for her help.

But we weren't quite done yet. Alice had a confession to make. It turns out Alice is very connected with Vikings. She has been to Iceland four times and visited all the Viking settlements she could locate. She wears a ring with a black Icelandic Viking stone in it. And she never misses an episode of the TV show Vikings. In fact, we both later discovered we had been Viking brothers in a few past lives.

Alice late told me how much my Viking brother loved me. She described his love for me as "immense".

Thank you my brother. I love you and I honor you. You are home now.

CHAPTER EIGHT
MY PERSONAL HEALING MIRACLE

It was a Monday night at the end of January 2013. Lying in bed with my wife, Karen, I suddenly couldn't breathe. I was coughing up fluid from my lungs; I just could not get a breath. This was a frightening, new experience for me. I grabbed my blood pressure monitor and my reading was off the charts. I asked Karen to call 911 while I grabbed a few things for the hospital. I was waiting outside for the ambulance because it was easier to breathe standing than sitting. The ambulance appeared at the same time as two police cars and a fire truck (which happened to take out my mailbox). I was loaded into the ambulance and the EMTs began inserting needles and prepping me for the emergency room. My blood pressure was through the roof. They thought I had congestive heart failure.

It took a few hours for the emergency room doctor to get me stabilized. He told me the next step was to find out why this happened. I could look forward to being in the hospital until they knew the cause of my heart incident.

The next two days were a blur of cardiac tests. I was wheeled into room after room, hooked up to dozens of electrodes, and put through numerous stress tests. Two days later I still didn't know what caused my incident. Then a new cause to worry appeared.

Karen and our son, Robbie, were visiting me Wednesday night when a small, neatly dressed man knocked at the door.

"Come in" I said, not recognizing the person.

"Hi! I'm your urologist" came his reply.

"Uh, I'm sorry, you must have the wrong room, I don't have a urologist" I replied.

"Well you do now" he said as he introduced himself to all of us. Then he asked Karen and Robbie to leave the room.

The doctor described how the CAT scan of my chest picked up a tumor on my left kidney. This tumor was very large and wrapped around the artery entering my kidney. He explained how this is the most common way of detecting these tumors, by accident. They don't cause pain, but once they do it's too late. He then told me I needed an operation to remove the tumor in the next month, and I may lose my kidney too.

My response to this news surprised the heck out of me. "OK, Doc, I have 2 kidneys, right? So I'll be fine" I heard myself say.

The doctor was surprised by my laid-back attitude regarding losing a major organ. "You'll be in the hospital for 4 days, then confined to bed for about 3 weeks. It takes at least 2 months for a full recovery" he explained to me.

"No problem" I heard myself say.

When the doctor left, Karen and Robbie came back into the room. I gave them the news. They didn't take it as well as I had. They were very concerned and crying.

It suddenly hit me that Spirit had put me in the hospital with a heart problem in order to find the bigger threat to my health, the kidney problem. And in my book, that meant I was going to be fine in both cases. I had full trust and faith in Spirit, but that didn't make my family feel any better about it.

Thursday morning my cardiologist said he wanted to repeat some tests because he didn't like the previous results. Uh oh, this was definitely not what I wanted to hear on my third day in the hospital. I repeated the tests, and saw my cardiologist again around dinner time. He didn't mince words.

"First thing in the morning I'm inserting a cardiac catheter into your heart so I can see what's going on in there. There may be blockages" he told me. Definitely not what I wanted to hear at all. In fact, now I was worried.

After he left the room, I grabbed my laptop and composed a short, to-the-point email to all the shamans I knew around the world, about 40 in all. I asked for their help in healing my heart, and to please start sending me healing energy immediately.

A few hours later I was in my room by myself when I began to feel it. The healing energy was hitting me in waves. I could feel each wave sweep over my body, fill me with a feeling I've never experienced before, and slowly recede. This went on for hours. I could see three points of light in one corner of my room, and I knew those lights were three angels overseeing the process. I eventually fell asleep, and not one nurse came in to check on me throughout the night. For the first time since I was admitted to the hospital, I had a good night's sleep.

When I was wheeled into the operating room for the cardiac catheter procedure, my cardiologist was waiting for me. He inserted the camera through my groin artery, and soon I was watching the camera cruise through the parts of my heart.

After a few minutes, I heard my cardiologist exclaim "Wow! I don't believe this!"

Uh oh, I thought, this can't be good. "What is it, Doc?" I asked.

"Your heart is perfect! Not a damn thing wrong!" he replied. That was music to my ears. My shaman friends came through for me in a BIG way that night.

Six hours later, after my groin artery recovered from the catheter, I was released from the hospital with a clean bill of health- well, except for the kidney tumor.

My cardiologist stated, with a smile on his face, that he never wanted to see me again, but I still had to deal with my kidney problem. While my urologist never used the "C" word (cancer), my wife and friends were convinced that is what the tumor was. I can honestly say I wasn't concerned about it. I knew deep down that Spirit had put me in the hospital to discover the kidney problem, and, as such, Spirit wasn't going to let me die from this. Of this I was certain.

The surgery was scheduled for early May. Again, I reached out to my shaman community for help and support, and

I know they were with me the entire time. In fact, one shaman said to me there were so many spirits and angels watching over the operation it was "standing room only."

Everything went so well, in fact, that I stopped using the pain medication in 36 hours and was released to go home after 72 hours. I had zero problems with the operation, and zero problems with the recovery. The tumor biopsy showed it was the big "C", but there were no traces of cancer in my body. I continue to be cancer-free to this day, and I know Spirit will keep me this way. I have a lot of healing and teaching work to do before I transition from this plane of existence.

Shamanic Depossession

54

REFERENCES

Allen, Sue. (2007). <u>Spirit Release: A practical handbook.</u> WInchester, UK; O Books.

Baldwin, WIlliam J. (2012). <u>Spirit Release Therapy.</u> Terra Alta, WV: Headline Books, Inc.

Baldwin, William J. (2003). Healing Lost Souls: Releasing unwanted spirits from your energy body. Charlottesville, VA: Hampton Roads Publishing Company, Inc.

Maurey, Eugene. (1988). <u>Exorcism: How to clear at a distance a spirit possessed person</u>. West Chester, PA: Whitford Press.

Sagan, Samuel MD. (1997). <u>Entity Possession: Freeing the body of negative influences.</u> Rochester, VT: Destiny Books.

The Foundation for Shamanic Studies- Dedicated to the preservation, teaching and study of shamanic knowledge for the welfare of the Planet and its inhabitants. Created by Michael Harner, author of "The Way of the Shaman" and the world's foremost expert on shamanism. www.shamanism.org

Down to Earth- The Shaman's Circle- Nan Moss and David Corbin. Originators of Weather Shamanism. My personal mentors. David is now with the great drum circle in the sky. I miss you David. www.shamanscircle.com

Betsy Bergstrom- Originator of Compassionate Depossession. www.betsybergstrom.com

Little Frog Healing- The author's healing practice website. www.littlefroghealing.com

Circle of the Sacred Earth Church- Shamanic church located in Melrose, MA. www.circleofthesacredearth.org

Circles of Air, Circles of Stone- Sparrow Hart's Vision Quest website. www.questforvision.com

ABOUT THE AUTHOR

Brad "Little Frog" Hudson is a well known shamanic practitioner and teacher, multidimensional energy healer, best selling author, and southern-style barbecue fanatic. His medicine name, "Little Frog", came from Spirit during his first Vision Quest, a four day/night solo fast in Vermont's Green Mountain wilderness. Spirit certainly has a sense of humor- Little Frog more closely resembles an NFL defensive tackle than a tiny amphibian.

Little Frog has always asked Spirit to bring him those people modern medicine can no longer help. He has helped many people who thought they would never experience relief from their problems. He works with people and animals, both locally and long distance. His shamanic and healing website is www.LittleFrogHealing.com.

Little Frog resides in Westford, Massachusetts with his wife, Karen, and son, Robbie.

Other books by Brad "Little Frog" Hudson:

Vision Quests: True Stories From the Wilderness

The Truth About You: Who You Are and Why You're Here on Earth

www.ingramcontent.com/pod-product-compliance
Lightning Source LLC
Chambersburg PA
CBHW031332040426
42443CB00005B/306